Searchlight BOOKS™

Cutting-Edge STEM

Cutting-Edge
Virtual Reality

Christy Peterson

Lerner Publications ◆ Minneapolis

For E^2 and J, who make my reality better every day

Content consultant: Erik Ness, Master Level Firmware Engineer

Lerner Publications Company
A division of Lerner Publishing Group, Inc.
241 First Avenue North
Minneapolis, MN 55401 USA

For reading levels and more information, look up this title
at www.lernerbooks.com.

Library of Congress Cataloging-in-Publication Data

The Cataloging-in-Publication Data for *Cutting-Edge Virtual Reality* is on file at the
    Library of Congress.
ISBN 978-1-5415-2347-0 (lib. bdg.)
ISBN 978-1-5415-2777-5 (pbk.)
ISBN 978-1-5415-2540-5 (eb pdf)

Manufactured in the United States of America
1-44420-34679-4/9/2018

Contents

Chapter 1

WHAT IS VIRTUAL REALITY?

Your hands grip the steering wheel. Cars on your left and right rev their engines. The light turns green, and you smash your foot into the gas pedal. The car leaps ahead. You screech around the first corner, tires smoking. Suddenly you hear a voice in your ear say, "Hey, it's my turn. Your time is up."

Some video games include equipment such as pedals and steering wheels so they seem more like real life.

This boy uses a headset and controller to play a virtual reality game.

You sigh. You were just about to take the lead! But you pull off the headset and hand the controls to your sister. Soon she is experiencing the car, the track, and the revving engines of a virtual reality racing game. You are stuck in your living room.

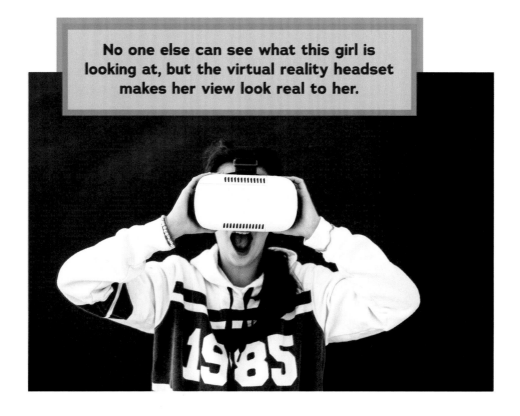

No one else can see what this girl is looking at, but the virtual reality headset makes her view look real to her.

What is a virtual reality game, and why does it feel so real? Reality is everything in the real world. We experience reality using our senses—smell, touch, taste, sight, and hearing. We also use our senses of balance and movement. *Virtual* means "close to being something without actually being it." A virtual reality system fools our senses. It makes us feel that we are experiencing something real when we are not.

How Does Virtual Reality Work?

To fool our senses, a virtual reality system needs two parts—software and hardware. Software is another word for a computer program. A program is a set of instructions that tells the computer how to create images and sounds. Software created that purple race car you've been driving. Want to change the color to yellow? The program tells the computer how to do that too.

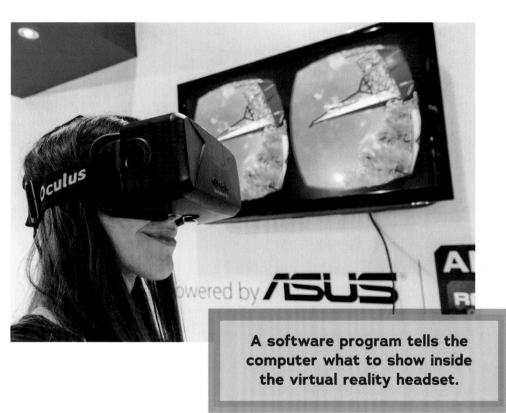

A software program tells the computer what to show inside the virtual reality headset.

A VIRTUAL REALITY HEADSET IS A PIECE OF HARDWARE.

▼

The program also tells the computer to send sounds and images to the hardware. Hardware is the parts of the system that you wear and hold. Some systems use a computer, headset, and controller. Others use a smartphone. The hardware sends information back to the program. Turn the controller too hard in your racing game, and the program sends your car off the track.

Coding Spotlight

A computer program is a set of instructions. Inside a computer, these instructions become binary code. This code tells the computer what to do using a series of yes-or-no questions. A yes answer becomes the number 1, which turns an electrical signal on. A no answer becomes 0, which turns the electrical signal off. An example of a yes-or-no question might be, "Is the player pressing the gas pedal button?" If yes, the car moves forward. If no, the car stays still.

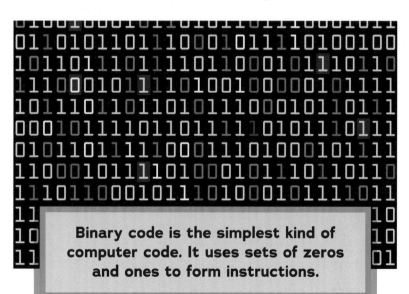

Binary code is the simplest kind of computer code. It uses sets of zeros and ones to form instructions.

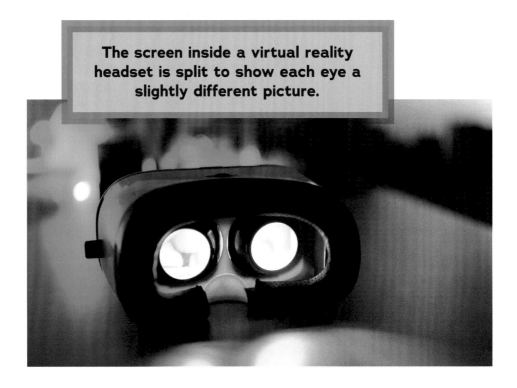

The screen inside a virtual reality headset is split to show each eye a slightly different picture.

Virtual reality feels real because the software and hardware work together. Inside a headset, the program creates a virtual world on the screen. Each eye sees a slightly different image, just as your eyes see two different images in real life. Your brain combines the two images to make one. This is how you see 3D.

The headset also tracks head movements. It tells the program to change the images on the screen when you turn your head. Speakers play sounds that go along with the images.

Chapter 2

CREATING VIRTUAL WORLDS

Many people enjoy playing *Minecraft*. Players use blocks to create landscapes, buildings, and towns. People first played *Minecraft* on flat computer screens or televisions. Later, programmers created a virtual reality version. How did they take a flat image on a screen and change it into a 3D world?

The video game *Minecraft* is popular around the world.

Imagine standing inside a ball. You look up, down, or side to side. No matter where you look, your view never comes to an edge. Imagine a *Minecraft* world drawn on the inside of the ball. This is how programmers create a virtual world. They place players in the center of an imaginary ball and draw the virtual world all around them. No matter where you look or how far you walk, you are always at the center of the ball, and the world never comes to an edge.

People tried out virtual reality *Minecraft* at an event in 2016.

The *Minecraft* world uses computer-generated imagery, or CGI. To create these objects and scenery, programmers start with basic shapes. In *Minecraft*, this is easy—everything is made of blocks! Programmers working on other games use many shapes to create a basic outline of an object. Slowly they mold these shapes into things like race cars or animals. They add colors and textures. Finally, they arrange the objects to create a scene.

The Universe from Your Living Room

Imagine your family is planning a vacation. Your sister wants to see New York City from the top of One World Trade Center. You want to watch a Formula One race. Virtual reality lets you check out these sights before you travel. Programmers re-create a real place just as they do an imaginary world. But instead of CGI, they place photos and videos inside the ball. You and your family can try out both experiences to see which one you might like to do in person.

A fan tries out a virtual reality headset during a Formula One race in England.

Science Fact or Science Fiction?

Using virtual reality programs for fun is a brand-new invention.

False.

About sixty years ago, Morton Heilig invented the Sensorama. Users sat in a seat and looked into a giant box. The machine took them on a wild motorcycle ride. As the scenery flew by on a screen, the seat rattled, and the virtual engine roared. A fan blew hair back, and vents sent out smells. The machine never caught on, and only a few were ever made.

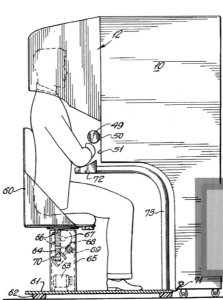

This illustration shows Heilig's plans for the Sensorama.

Virtual reality also opens the world to people who might not be able to travel. One experience combines thousands of images and sounds from Mount Everest. People hear the crunch of the snow and see stunning views from the top of the mountain. Virtual reality can even take you out of this world. You can try living in a Mars colony or walking on the moon.

Have you ever dreamed of visiting Mars? One virtual reality game lets you explore the planet and search for signs of life.

Chapter 3

VIRTUAL REALITY AT WORK

Virtual reality isn't just fun and games. One early tool taught people how to fly planes. Edwin Link used piano and organ parts to build a training machine, or simulator, about ninety years ago. The simulator had airplane controls, and it tilted and rolled. Students learned what it felt like to fly before operating a real plane.

Members of the French Air Force train on a Link simulator in 1941.

This flight simulator includes all the controls and instruments that would be in a real plane.

The military still uses simulators to teach soldiers how to operate planes, tanks, ships, and even submarines. These simulators create virtual reality experiences. For the soldier, the machine feels like the real thing. A computer program plays video and sounds. Simulators allow soldiers to practice in a safe place before going to the battlefield.

Science Fact or Science Fiction?

Virtual reality can make you sick.

That's true!

When what we see doesn't match our movement, we sometimes get dizzy or feel sick. In virtual reality, there is a time gap between moving your head in the real world and the virtual image catching up. Some game creators have chosen to slow things down and make motion less smooth, with turns happening in short chunks. This helps players feel more comfortable because it is easier for the brain to process the motion.

Virtual Reality Saves Lives

In 2017, a medical team separated twins whose bodies were joined at the heart. The team planned the risky surgery with the help of virtual reality. Doctors wore virtual reality glasses to look at 3D images of the girls' hearts. They even walked inside the hearts! This allowed them to plan the safest way to operate.

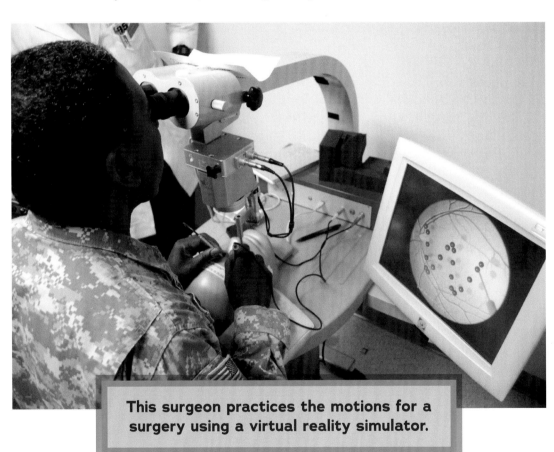

This surgeon practices the motions for a surgery using a virtual reality simulator.

THIS PERSON TRIES OUT A VIRTUAL REALITY SURGERY SIMULATOR AT A TECHNOLOGY SHOW IN 2016.

▼

Virtual reality is a useful training tool for emergency room staff. Instead of practicing on plastic dummies, teams train using virtual reality headsets. They feel the stress of an actual emergency and become more prepared to help patients in a real situation.

An astronaut completes a space walk during a
mission on the International Space Station.

Expect the Unexpected

High above Earth, you work to repair a broken satellite.
A thick cord attaches you to your spaceship. One by
one, you remove bolts so you can reach the damaged
part. Suddenly disaster strikes. The cord detaches
from the ship. You are floating free in space. What will
you do?

Carefully, you use tiny jets in your backpack to steer your way back to the ship. But you weren't really lost in space. You were in an astronaut-training program. NASA uses virtual reality to teach astronauts how to live and work in space. Astronauts practice dealing with the unexpected. This helps them stay safe when they go on real space missions.

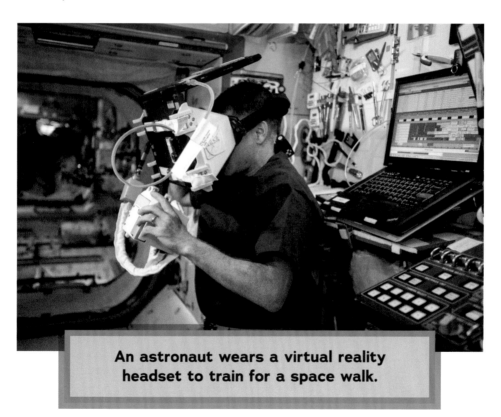

An astronaut wears a virtual reality headset to train for a space walk.

Chapter 4

A BRIGHT FUTURE

Virtual reality can make us feel we are someone else or somewhere else. This is helpful in surprising ways. At a museum in Ohio, you can use virtual reality to become Rosa Parks, an African American woman who fought for equal rights for people of different races. In the virtual reality experience, you climb aboard a bus after a long workday. Then someone orders you to give your seat to someone else, just because of your race. Through virtual reality, you can understand how other people might feel and why they do things.

Rosa Parks

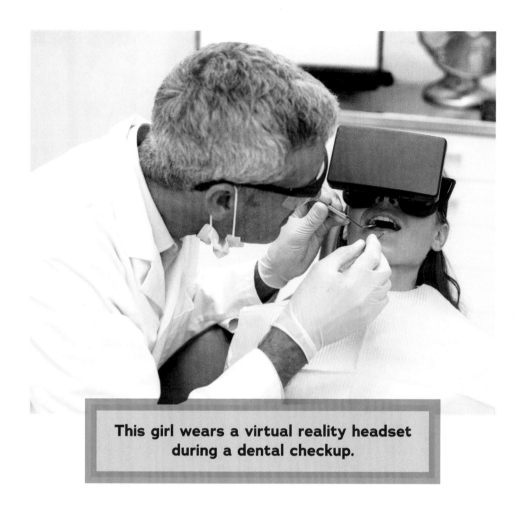

This girl wears a virtual reality headset during a dental checkup.

Another program makes a visit to the dentist less scary. Patients strap on a virtual reality headset while they sit in the dentist's chair. Instead of focusing on the whine of a dentist's drill or the sharp tools the dentist is using, they can walk along a beach or through a forest. Having a pleasant virtual experience helps the patients feel less pain.

Virtual Reality in Action

Virtual reality tools are helping paraplegics. These people can't move their lower bodies because of an illness or accident. Using a tool connected to the brain, a patient thinks about how to move a virtual person across an imaginary field. The tool measures the patient's brain activity to send signals to the virtual person. This helps a patient's brain relearn how to send signals to the legs to move.

What scares you? Virtual reality can help you overcome fear. Imagine your biggest fear is high places. A virtual reality program takes you to the top of a tall building. Little by little, you approach the edge of a balcony. Then you walk out on a platform ten stories up. Facing fears virtually helps us respond more calmly in real life.

Many people become nervous, dizzy, or shaky when they look out of tall buildings. Virtual reality programs can teach them to feel calm and safe.

Virtual Reality—Full Speed Ahead

The senses we use to experience virtual worlds are mostly sight and hearing. Developers are working on virtual reality suits that let you feel things in a virtual world. But many people want a virtual experience that includes all the senses. Imagine a virtual reality trip to Antarctica where you can smell the fresh, cool air. You pick up snow and feel cold. You even taste snow melting on your tongue.

WHAT DO YOU THINK ANTARCTICA SMELLS, FEELS, AND TASTES LIKE?

Computer programmers work every
day to create new and exciting
programs and experiences.

We're not there yet, but faster computers and
better programs are allowing virtual reality to be part
of our lives in new and exciting ways. One day you
might have virtual reality experiences that no one has
even imagined yet.

Glossary

binary code: the most basic computer language made up of a series of 0s and 1s

computer-generated imagery (CGI): images of objects and landscapes created by a computer program

computer program: a set of instructions that tells a computer how to do a task

paraplegic: a person who cannot move the lower body due to an illness or accident

programmer: a person who writes instructions that tell a computer what to do

simulator: a machine used for training that mimics a real tool

surgery: a medical process that usually involves operating on or inside a person's body

3D: short for three-dimensional. An object that is 3D has height, width, and depth.

virtual reality headset: a tool worn on the head that puts a user in a virtual world

Learn More about Virtual Reality

Books

Bodden, Valerie. *Virtual Reality Headsets*. Minneapolis: Checkerboard Library, 2018. Read more about the history of virtual reality and the ways it is used.

Challoner, Jack. *Virtual Reality*. New York: DK, 2017. Find out more about virtual reality, and try it out for yourself.

Peterson, Christy. *Cutting-Edge Augmented Reality*. Minneapolis: Lerner Publications, 2019. Learn about another amazing technology that looks a lot like virtual reality but is used in different ways.

Websites

Explain That Stuff: Virtual Reality
http://www.explainthatstuff.com/virtualreality.html
Check out this website to learn more about different types of virtual reality as well as its history and uses.

Minecraft
https://minecraft.net/en-us/vr/
Check out this website and video to see what virtual reality *Minecraft* is like.

Wonderopolis: What Is Virtual Reality
https://wonderopolis.org/wonder/what-is-virtual-reality
Read more about virtual reality, watch a video, and try out some activities to understand this technology.

Index

Photo Acknowledgments

Image credits: guruXOOX/Getty Images, p. 4; stockfour/Shutterstock.com, p. 5; Carol Yepes/
Moment/Getty Images, p. 6; Tinxi/Shutterstock.com, p. 7; SAQUIZETA/Shutterstock.com,
p. 8; Jason Winter/Shutterstock.com, p. 9; leungchopan/Shutterstock.com, p. 10; Bloomicon/
Shutterstock.com, p. 11; Gabrielle Lurie/AFP/Getty Images, p. 12; gilaxia/Getty Images,
p. 13; Jack Taylor/Getty Images, p. 14; U.S. Patent #3050870, p. 15; NASA/JPL, pp. 16, 22,
23; Central Press/Hulton Archive/Getty Images, p. 17; Paulo Fridman/Corbis/Getty Images,
p. 18; izusek/Getty Images, p. 19; Lorin T. Smith/Army Medicine/Madigan Army Medical
Center, p. 20; Jean-Francois Monier/AFP/Getty Images, p. 21; Bettmann/Getty Images, p. 24;
Wavebreakmedia/Getty Images, p. 25; Photographee.eu/Shutterstock.com, p. 26; MarynaG/
Shutterstock.com, p. 27; Jan Miko/Shutterstock.com, p. 28; Hero Images/Getty Images, p. 29.

Cover: slavemotion/Getty Images.